THIS IS NOT A POEM

Poems

Richard Inya

Edited by Nsah Mala

Mwanaka Media and Publishing Pvt Ltd,
Chitungwiza Zimbabwe
*
Creativity, Wisdom and Beauty

Publisher: Mmap
Mwanaka Media and Publishing Pvt Ltd
24 Svosve Road, Zengeza 1
Chitungwiza Zimbabwe
mwanaka@yahoo.com
www.africanbookscollective.com/publishers/mwanaka-media-and-publishing
https://facebook.com/MwanakaMediaAndPublishing/

Distributed in and outside N. America by African Books Collective
orders@africanbookscollective.com
www.africanbookscollective.com

ISBN: 978-0-7974-9336-0
EAN: 9780797493360

© Richard Inya 2019

DISCLAIMER
All views expressed in this publication are those of the author and do
not necessarily reflect the views of *Mmap*.

Table of Contents

DISQUIET

LEAVING

EARTH

LIVING

TONGUES AND FIRE

TERROR

Marianne Van der Wel and Macpherson Okpara
Take this, kindest of hearts, for what we believe is true

FOREWORD

A poet is not just a voice of whimsical fantasy, but a prophet and a seer. He is not just a whimsical dreamer singing in the market place, but a thinker and a catalyst for change. His voice mirrors the provocateur and the soothsayer all in one breath. Like Anansi, the spider that inspired the first kente cloth, the poet inspires the fabric of the future. Richard Inya is bold and fearless, characteristics embodied by his mantra, 'This is not a poem.' He lays claim to the validity and authority of the poet and poetry to critique society in every dimension, including its politics.

Africa is at crossroads; it is truly a critical time, a time for our thinkers to stand up with boldness. Indeed it is time for the poet to make his voice heard. With his opening lines under Disquiet, the poet sets the somberness of tone with deliberate intent. The brevity of the lines serves as emphasis. The first poem launches the offensive: in a satirical tongue, the poet takes on the vice of corruption, ineptitude of service, etc. Using bold, blunt language, he attacks social ills like violence, greed and hypocrisy, among others. The poem, 'Crying in the Rain' captures the poet's bitter disappointment with political ideologies that fail to address the needs of citizens.

Using brevity again as a stylistic device, the poet calls attention to a different theme, putting the spotlight on young people searching elsewhere for home and destiny, appealing to seasoned minds to revoke their exile and return to the land of their forefathers in order to rebuild what is broken.

There is something of the polemic in the unflinching lines, running together though separate and distinct, from the first line to the last, challenging notions of useless mysteries as advanced by critics such as George Steiner, fearlessly advocating the concept that poetry does indeed serve purposeful functionality.

NyamburaKiarie,
Kibage, Kenya

PREFACE

A poet, to me, is like someone whose house is by the roadside. One whose dwelling is along the road should not be tired of acknowledging rounds of greetings. So, a poet should not be tired of rising in condemnation of social ills and other ugly situations in his society. He should devote his craft to the betterment of his people, to the overall happiness and wellbeing of mankind. This might be the reason most poets recognise silence as a heavier burden. Thus, they lend their voices, penning in reaction to unhealthy occurrences.

However, it often happens that when a poet rises to express genuine concern for his society through lines that represent streams of tears, the poetry of those lines is appreciated more than the issues raised. Such issues are lost to the appreciation of the art. *My tears are called poetry by those who love to see me cry.* The poet becomes a man crying in the rain; only he sees his tears.

This work is not an outrage. It is not an expression of despair or anxiety; it is an attempt to foreground the things that shrink our capacity to excel, that milk us dry as a people, and block us from the light of honour and glory. This is about the things that give rise to incessant abduction of school girls, the things that make us live in fear, the things that make the sane blurt out in anger and frustration: Why can't politics be played peacefully? Why can't we manage our God-given resources to the benefit of all? Aren't we blessed enough to better our lot with our hands and ideas so that our people would stop dying in their numbers in an attempt to run away to better countries through the desert and the sea? Why can't we stop valorising greed, notoriety and corruption in the name of politics and affluence?

Far from outrage or despair, this volume contains verses that embody disappointment and regrets. If democracy is the government of the people, the people should benefit more from it. If we are blessed with vast mineral resources, our standard of living should improve. If the youths are the future leaders of our country, they should be adequately equipped with quality education. All these are not quite happening. Sadly, no corner is secure anymore, except in the quarters of they that short-circuit the common good and well-being of the people, those for whom the air of insecurity translates into its physical equivalence: bags of hard currencies. The woes of this land cannot be reduced to poetry. No, this is not a poem.

Richard Inya

2019

DISQUIET

. . . My tears are called poetry
By those who love to see me cry
- Richard Inya (From *Katakata*)

IN THE REALM OF SERVICE

An armed revolution
Rages against quietness
In the belly of starving ones

Their intestines are trapped snakes
Struggling to break loose
Ever seen they that chew silence and swallow air?

Pity is a bucketful of moments of silence
Harvested from the bosom of caretakers
Who wait to cast oration on graveyards

Promises trick despair
Vain promises are faecal stuff
From the anus of bloated talks

This path is not far from mass murder
Another has just fallen
Whose statue will never make it into the square

IN THE REALM OF SERVICE (2)

At the end of service
Is a houseful of ghosts
Echoes and questions

Should I go or should I stay?
What if tomorrow doesn't come
Or hunger lifts me away?

Fifty something is allergic to jokes on age
Where trepidation begets rejuvenation
In the enclave of browning records
Manipulation hands out extra years
To faces ripe to vacate the facade of duty

Retirement songs echo the sounds of war with self
The sphere of service is a mountain village
Every swift leap or brisk walk awaits accounting
When age meets with the year of reckoning

IN THE REALM OF SERVICE (3)

Giant hawks prey on pension funds
Hawks are rock-hearted caretakers
Nay, lions watching over aged sheep

Out in the cold the old queue
The lot of retirees exalts beggars
And sets the feet of the fledgling
On the path of wanton thievery

The piteous lot of veterans
Is the offence of tribesmen
Tongues and facial marks hide them

The wellbeing of the aged is the Holy Grail
The search for this is endless
Arthritis accompanies spent legs
On their way to verification
There shall be more and more roll calls
Until the hawks fly with the records

SCATTERED

Oneness has taken flight
Like dew overpowered
By the sun's manly face
So is commonality gone

Another's corpse is a log
The tears of the bereaved
Are streams of misty fancy
Before mirthless consolers

The blood of innocence
Is adrift in a violent flow
Life is only a mushroom
The meal of termites

We are now like aged drunks
Admiring pallbearers' wears
And funeral songs are lullabies
To the children of the unaffected

We are flies trapped in a keg
Of raffia wine; a stranded
Species lonely in its crowd

A multitude swept into solitude

We'd swear and curse and brood
And sue if a car crushes a dog
We don't care to tell the children
A mad man is someone else's son

We are oil-bean pods shattered
By the hand of an angry wind
Each freed seed journeys abroad
Into the belly of wandering ones

We are a sea of blind eyes that won't see
That unshared laughter weakens the teeth?

HOW SHOULD I REMEMBER YOU?

Have they conquered you?
Are you now a grief-stricken one
Gowned with a cloak of gloom
Like a bride jilted on her wedding day?
Have they conquered you?

Have safety-conscious travellers
Bypassed your roads like a house
Full of paranormal presence?
Are you now a militant ghost lurking around?
A deadly fugitive hounded for a pay?
Ominous sounds at the backdrop of night?

They have named you by the things of death
You are now a dusty shadow playing pranks
A loud sepulchral voice feigning hurt
A site for mass burial of fallen ones
A ghoulish air fanning up bloodshed
The entrance of a deserted cemetery
Suspicious bereaved calling for séance
They have named you by the things of death

I see you in the eyes of your maidens

Such grace as beauty given to the beautiful
I have eaten your food and drunk of your river
I see you in the contoured bodies of lively ones
Jigging, twisting to the sounds of happy drums
I see you in your cat dancers

When the dust of terror settles
And the billows of rage recede
When requiem songs cease to be lullabies
And the strings of safety are tied again
Please tell me, glorious home of ripe things
How should I remember you?

A TIME TO GRAB

Look up
They are in the sky
Flying back into our circle
Let every eye follow them

Where are the broad-chested?
Where are the muscular ones?
Where are the fingers that love triggers?
Where are those with nocturnal credentials?
Where are the addicts to cash and strong wine?

Volleyed cash bags are airborne
Floating like hot-air balloons
Returning to our square
Look up

Flaunt your manhood, loose ones
The season of decadence is here
What's denied the people is back
Grab your cut and stride to opulence

Rejoice, fair ladies of fleshy zones
Fling open the doors that shield your beds
If nudity is your battledress, wear it
Why should one bother how a fair lady sits?
Who knows from which part breeze
Makes ingress into her bosom?

Fling open your doors, fair ladies
Twist your waists and wait
For whatever is released to thugs is yours
Thuggery is the expressway to quick riches
Yours is a safer bank

The days of bazaar are near
Can you smell the Christmassy fragrance?
Stand in the middle, brace up and wait
What's denied the people is back
Grab your cut and stride to opulence

Rejoice, hapless voters
The harmattan fog of lack
Shall take a casual leave
When the cash bags drop

But who has ever fed fat on stolen food?
What the ear calls a sweet sound
The tongue knows as a bitter taste

He that cheats on food
Spends more time in the toilet

SEARCHING

Kites I have seen
Return from faraway coasts

Dragonflies I have seen
Tasting waters

Glow-worms I have seen
Searching for the night

Beetles I have seen
Rolling balls of mud

Ravens I have seen
Dancing for the wind

Tadpoles I have seen
Squirming to growth

Old people I have seen everywhere
Elders I cannot find

THIS SHALL PASS

Every face now is a loud placard
Yours, your mother's and mine
Drizzling tears are emblems of ebbing hope
Hope struggles like confetti caught in a whirlwind

We are a weighty pebble fighting
To stay afloat upon a murky pool
There's harmattan in every throat
And thorns in every word
We speak in loud sighs and silence

The boom of doom is a scary tale in the North
At South's tail is a fusillade of lethal shots
Echoing the rhythms of militancy in the hearts of men
Quartered behind the mangroves

At every corner here in the birthplace
Of my forefathers are yawning mouths
Hurling magnetic words to attract alms
The products of their effort walk like a mother
Held up in the pang of contraption

Who can tell the sharers of our national sauce

That pleasantries equal insult to an unfed mouth?
How would they know the wind has rejected their songs?
Yet the colour of things bright and flowering
Speaks to my heart: This shall also pass

CRYING IN THE RAIN

See what we've become
My anguish is a melody
I'm a man crying in the rain
None sees my tears but me

Didn't you know I was in the field
When you asked the cloud to gather
And the rain to come?
How well it is with the comfortable

There's nothing left to see
If the ocean boils over
Raging through life's embankment
Or stones fly up against the moon
We would smile like we'd seen it before

See what we've become
Tears could be canned for export
I'm a man crying in the rain
None sees my tears but me

STRIPS OF DOUBT

Is this you rolling noisily
Like a meatless snail shell?
Is this all of you?

At the dawn of your arrival
Hearty mouths called you
Open heaven and a voice
Today you speak stormy words
Spitting nails into faces

Many served their lives in trays
You took, ate and returned emptiness
Did we sell a dog just to buy a monkey?
Flashes of light have killed more than bullets
The bullets we escaped from to hide in your skin

Suspicion is our new creed and anthem
Every bird is a spy; whatever that flies is a drone
War songs are alarm tones for our devices
War songs are moonlight songs for our kids
Dangerous beasts are our cherished totems
You bade us speak in our choice tongues
There came a rain of curses and aspersions

We are like a child tired of running chores

When a child becomes tired of running chores
He equally becomes ready to fight everyone
We are prodigal children calling our lot freedom
A child that does not know that the hydrocele
Between his father's legs is a disease
Often craves for a lump of meat as large as the hydrocele
We are lost children in the forest of freedom
You bade us speak in our choice tongues
And there came a rain of curses and aspersions
You bade us build, and a tower sprang up in Babel
You bade us lead, and a few stole the way
They sweep aside exotic things for themselves
Many bear the burden of silence, awaiting a miracle

Despair. Deceit. Denial
Is this all you can be, newfound freedom?
Is this you rolling noisily
Like a meatless snail shell?
Is this all of you?

RUNNING

Your non-Igboness confuses me
Young Deltan canoeing upon a sea
Of twisted figures, tales and names
Your father's name hosts our deity
That no longer shares our libation
Your tongue is my father's tongue
The words you bite, chew and spew
Into the turbulent belly of the Niger

You shade your face from ancestral rays
And snub the warmth of the rising sun
Your heart courses with the rivers
Picking up tongues that call differently
What you should know by our tongue
We call you water; you call yourself oil
You are not one in yourself

The throat of the sea can be parched
An oil drum can yield to rust, dear son
Of estranged rivers running to the sea
Pray, take lessons in your mother tongue
Learn to blame death before blaming vultures
We all are one with the cords of our root

FITFUL FATE

We are trees
Home of monkeys
When monkeys cough
The trees cough
We know not rest

We are banana trees
Bearers of sweet things
We need monkeys
That do not like banana

GIVE OVER

They sang that when you come
Sons of the night shall run from light
Behold, darkness has conquered you

You are a wishful fire dreaded in error
Your atrophied righteousness
Like caked blood on the slain
Leaves dark spots on the scene

Review the mind of your sacred mission
For faith writhes around and hope billows
With the smoke of lack and mendacity
Pray give over, cold fire, be gone

Our patrimony now is cannabis farm
Pens walk on dotted spaces in your name
Why should a tired dancer call for more drumming?
Pray give over, cold fire, cease

Your face is patterned after the blazing sun
You blink when cowards stare into your eyes
They wish your reign grips firmly till forever comes
But we pray you give over, cold fire, be gone

FRAGMENTS

She parrots at her backyard
Before her tender ones
'Those other children are not us
For we are the great pots
That can't be carried to the stream
We are the centre of this land
No kid in this land equals you'

Her words offer other kids kola nuts
And they are broken into lobes
Each lobe is a hand tugging at the land
They lay claim
They hear what they want to hear
And the fortunate tell them more

SERVING

Thunder claps for the moon
That dares glow in the rain
Larks sing for they that come off
The mud of service clean

We hail. We wail
We call names
We are cannibals
We eat names

LEAVING

. . . Arid paths are slippery roads
Survivors are deep scars
Homes for sad memories

SCATTERED LONGINGS

The water over there is a mirror
Take a look at yourself
At the bottom of the sea

You are strands of seaweeds
Posing for marauding lives
Oblivion is around the dying

Your spirit speaks to your dreams
And the sound reaches Agadez
There is a thing about you in Tripoli
But your body borders Italy

The Sahara sun fleeced your skin
Like a sheep sheared for wool
The sky bullied your desire
Yet you beat all to the sea

Your father's eyes are glued to the skyline
Your mother's neck is longer than the sea
Expectations often are more on travellers
But only divers speak to sailing bodies

GOING DOWN

I saw scores of young faces
In the throes of drowning
Their strokes towards survival
Like the dance of dolphins
Leap, reaching for the sun

The sea is a restive gourmand
Swallowing up dreamers
Taking ambitious ones
 Into its cheerless embrace

I saw scores of young fellows
Abandoning their land of birth
Floating like waste on water
Going where the sea leads

UNCHECKED DREAM

You are a parcel of fat dreams
Strapped with a rope of feathers
Tied to the tail of a hurricane
Speeding to the Mediterranean

Unchecked dream is a violent wind
Unbridled ambition is a lint in the storm
Dreams are half-broken earthenware
Where desperate thoughts breed

You are a body bag waiting to be claimed
Body bags are dreams searching for a nation
You are Moses
There lies your promised land
That is Spain
This is Morocco
There is Europe
Here is Africa

Here you sail swollen-bellied like dead fish
In a poisoned pond showing off its belly to the sun
How would your brothers learn
That unchecked dream is a violent wind
That unbridled ambition is a lint in the storm?

CHAINED IN LIBYA

Fine-plumed egrets
Scorn food in the wetland
Now with ruffled feathers
Lose each day to aridity

You all are egrets
Shooed away by anxiety
You trudge each day
Under the weight of scorn

The chains of slavery
Jingle across the desert
Clanging to the pleasure of your brothers

Nubian tongues have no ears
Where vultures mock bedraggled owls
If colour and tongue wear the cloak of warning
How are you one with your assailants?

If you have tears in your eyes
Cry until they join the Nile
You're trapped at the corridor of torture
How are you one with your assailants?

ECHOES OF LEAVING

My mother's sons are migratory birds
Reaching for spaces in faraway coasts
High-spirited delight comes with tales
Gleeful expectations efface memories
Of things owned at home, of calls to stay

See how my mother's sons lie stretched
See how the sun plunders them like a game
Caught, skewered and given to fire

The dunes are graves for sojourners
Torpedoed in a sea of burning sand
Ridges of sand are high walls blocking
Hurried dreams from taking flesh
More are leaving their homelands
To be soon counted among the dead

PARCHED

Have the elements conspired against you?
Didn't you know air and earth
Are friends with fire?
Haven't you learnt water hides
From desert travellers?

Your eyes go faraway
Where the sky blends with the sand
But the water you seek is in your body

TURN AND RETURN

Desert routes receive donors for the sea
Arid paths are slippery roads
Survivors are deep scars
Homes for sad memories

Turn, return; my people, return
Our faggots can cook us food
A people's firewood cooks their food
Our wood burns well
Even if smoke enters your eyes
What's ours is ours

Each log is a promise
Hear the logs crackle in the fire
Hear the efforts of our hands speak
Each log is a promise
Turn, return; my people, return
Our faggots can cook us food

EARTH

. . .Make not light of the grave
For the earth fights her cause

LIVE FOR TOMORROW

They that harry the earth
Give their dwellings away
And bid rodents come home
Wherefore their abode is gone
Owls thus take flight at noontide

Sojourn not among those
That treasure snake soup
If their traps catch snakes
Let them savour the soup
If snakes catch their heels
Let them bear with herbal water

Make not light of the grave
For the earth fights her cause
Congregate not among the tribes
That call lightning flashes of light
For such tongues harry the earth

If the earth doesn't fight her cause
Why does lightning speak vile words?
Why does thunder raise his voice?
Why does the cloud break into tears?
Why does the rainbow seldom intervene?

The earth fights her cause

Tomorrow is heavy with our baby
Would we smile if it looked like us?
Not only a drunk tells his only son
One must get lost to learn new roads

Today's rat should not be burnt
Inside tomorrow's fair castle
Tomorrow is the today that stays
I speak not of men and pregnancies
But of the future that awaits the earth

SMOKY BREATH

Earth's grave roots deep in the cloud
It is dug by the agency of our hands
As the fart of labouring engines howl
And swirl with the fumes of industry

Our throats are parched by smoky air
We are drenched in our saliva
We raise our faces heavenward
Spitting at the quiet sky

If the earth folds away under our feet
Or mountains duff their tops for the sky
If we wake up to see the cloud is gone
That would be the deed of our hands

ANGRY SUN

The sky is a furnace
Of angry sun
Fighting for felled trees
Crying in the fire

Each branch that falls
Fuels the rage of the heat
Each twig that chars
Is a tongue of the vengeful fire

Any tree that comes down
Finds the eye of the earth
What eye stays calm
But one yet to gulp dust?

Trees are the lid of the sun
Say this to haters of the green
Who war against forests

LEAVE TO LIVE

Rivers gulp up the rains
Swelling like a python
After a swallow
Charging, they go as to war
With dwellers in the low plains
And the cries after are of losses

Vacate, brothers
Run to the highlands
What inheritance does the sane
Share with the irate flood?

Flood is a restless brute
A madman in a nightmare
Throwing punches in all directions
Making haste to nowhere

A patrimony on the path of the flood
Is but a fruit for one short season
For only the living tell life's tale
The mad make war with shadows
Angry waters are shadows of pain

Move up to higher ground, brothers

On the path of the flood lie losses
No mother eats her children in famine
Only the living tell life's tale

LUMBERMAN

Your machines like wild dogs
Run amok through the forests
Stampeding trees to death
Letting the sun touchdown

The cries of the trees jar through
The woods, disorienting species
Into extinction; the sun doubles
The ferocity of its sworn vengeance

Your progress is akin to two fowls
Carrying one cockroach
Nay, it's the lot of a bird perching on a line
Dancing to the tune of restlessness

The sun rests on our rooftops
Baring its body to every eye
Many a thing that lived is gone
And cool breeze is now luxury

ARMY OF WATERS

A gloomy sky is a curse on them
That dwell on the waterfront
They drink of the bitterness
Of the gourd handed them by the flood

The efforts of settlers are like a startled
Gecko in an enclosed space, running
Everywhere, running to nowhere
The end of the flood doesn't end its pains

The hearts of the affected are dim
As they mull over their perennial curse
Gazing everywhere for healing
The end of the flood doesn't end the pains

SWEEPING FLOW

The fire of flood melts the heart
Of they that heed not its signs
Their homes grant water thoroughfare
The daggers of rain hit the knob
Exuberant waters enlarge the coast
Of sweeping flow, everything rides
On the back of the flood to the sea

The heady on the path of the flood
Is a scarecrow dancing in the wind
The loot of the flood is enjoyed by the sea
And they that block its way pay tenfold

Let they that open the cage not bemoan
The flight of the bird
Heed and leave the path of the flood

DUMP SITES

A mountain of refuse
Stood in our way
Like traffic wardens
Motioning passersby
To alternate routes

Frenzied wind
Scatter rubbish
Hither, thither
Enveloping households
With dust and lint

Maggot mill undisturbed
Garbage trucks besieged by flies
Who knows the name
Of the next epidemic
That may ravage the city?

LIVING

. . . Everything leaves that lives
We shall like leaves leave

PEACE IS A CLOAK

When hate rents your mind
Peace scurries to a corner
Dying gradually like a great idea
Buried in an unpopular journal

How breathes an angry man
Who rubs faeces on his wears
To foul the air for his enemies?

Hate wears the face of the setting sun
There is often a splash of grudge
On the face of the setting sun
Amplified by those traces of faded purple

A loving heart is a serene pond
Calm, spacious, alluring
Giving no one a reason to hide
Behind their palms in shame

TEXTURE OF SELF

If your shadow comes after you with a gun
Do not run into the dark and hide
Just drop the gun in your hand

If darkness dares the efflorescence of your light
Go back and cast your skin like a snake
For yours is the toga of darkness

COST OF LEAVING

Everything leaves that lives
We shall like leaves leave
Leaving traces of our deeds
Sour, bitter or sweet aftertaste

Tend to every heart with love
So none shall leave with wounds

WE ARE ONE

We are ensnared bush fowls
We cry not that what holds us
Should free us
But that the world
Might hear our cry

Taunt not our lot
All you home birds
For tomorrow is still pregnant
All that have feathers are one

SILENCE IS A BURDEN

Something is wrong with 'all is well'
Long faces lynch pleasantries
The unspoken is still the loudest

I see long faces
Behind the veils of smile
Veins zigzagging beneath the skin
I am the quiet wall
I know the underbelly of a gecko

Let not a snake cut into two
Think of itself as two
I see veins wriggling like earthworms
Visited with grains of salt

I see long faces everywhere
I know private woes kill privately

UNBEAUTIFUL

My eyes follow you each day
Into your future
Your fingers are artists
Turning your face into a colour tray
Your eyelashes are peacocks
Your face is a colourful mask
 Nay, a costume for appealing
To cry-babies in the crèche

Your art is the act of swallowing time
Causing sweet things to taste like sour sausages
What makes a beautiful woman beautiful?
Your future races with the speed of a ceiling-fan
Making haste at one point
Yours is not reckoned as beautiful
Lest poetry be ascribed to the words of a pestle
Coming down on a mortar in anger
Yours is not beautiful
Beauty is not yours
For the face in the mirror is not yours

TONGUES AND FIRE

. . . That man is a child in stringing yarns
The one parroting that all paintings are idols

SHARP TONGUES

In the house of tongues and fire
A worshipper is a talkative man
Speaking strangeness to his father
Running to his mother to be born again

Words come scattering
Like a torn string of beads
Flung against a wall
The wall of the hall of Babel
Tongues of throngs babbling aloud

A man is taken from God
Given to tongues
Given to man
Given to blood
Given to fire
Left stranded like an infant
Pointing where he feels is the way home

That man is a child in stringing yarns
The one parroting that all paintings are idols
The one making haste to escape from his skin
These tongues are sharp objects
Keen blades cutting brotherly ties

CASH AND CARRY

A gale of wealth craze
Tears through the sanctuary
And the calling of the called
Is called to question

Who said God did not abscond
On the night they sculptured Him
In their image and likeness?

God is a tree of hard currencies
Standing under the soft sun
Bidding the anointed pluck

They pluck, great men of god
Nay, powerful gods of men
They pluck, leaving their god naked

IN SEARCH OF GOD

When you go on pilgrimage
The land lies quiet like a pond at night
And peace is the song of the people
Nursing the pains from your ceaseless loot

Do you wear stolen apparels to the holy land?
Do holy artefacts tremble at your holy feet?
How does yours differ from a picnic, O pilgrim?
Why does peace flee on your return?

We see your clasped holy hands
And slow-motioned steps to the altar
You receive God, you swallow God
But your being does not bulge with good

Yours is cosmetic holiness
You should reread Paul's letters
Let your being bulge with goodness
Whenever you swallow God

MALL OF GOD

Build you first the man
Before building the church
Lest he destroys himself
In destroying the church

At the confluence of man
And god is your empire
Your fruitful enterprise
Flourishing in god's name

Your strategy is biological warfare
Every word is a germ attacking
The pockets of unwilling donors

You give my sisters god to eat
You give them blood to drink
You are drenched in a rain of cash
For god's parts are yours for sale

Where would my sisters go
If the road to your heaven leads to hell?

TERROR

. . . Heads roll from low places to palaces
And we are inconsolable mourners

BESIEGED

I'm a den
Of reptiles
Do not wonder
Why all the frenzy
Pythons are dancing
Crocodiles are smiling
Be wary of these new drums
They beat the music of the dead
These drums are hewn from human skin
To remind the land whose conquered mother it is
Do not pretend you have not heard these sounds before
Who doesn't know sex on the beach is not new to the sand?

MASS BURIAL

A rain of nails
Falls on the coffins
Of the fallen
And we are vessels
Sailing on a sea of tears

Cows are trains
Who dares stand in their way?
Cows swallow souls
And graze wildly on graveyards

When these quietened ones are laid
In the womb of the earth
Ask yourself as you shuffle through this canvas
Where now is home?

ECHOES OF BRUTALITY

Brutality knows our given-names
And calls us out at every turn
There's a hole in the head of a man
Asking for his piece of communal cake

I saw some men blocking the growth of a man
Brutality is the disease of the powerful
The silence of the weak does not heal it

Those men rode on the trunks of toads
That man is a tadpole that mustn't croak
Do not cry for the man; cry for the land

SERVED TO COWS

We see heads roll each day
Like golf balls into holes
Each head is the future
Pulled backward and measured
With bad clocks and sighs
How dirty socks destroy elegant feet!

Heads roll from low places to palaces
And we are inconsolable mourners
We whose people are yam tubers
Reserved for unfettered goats
A brood for routine invasion by kites
We are the ones served daily to cows

VIOLENT INGRESS

How many words
Would be too much
To talk about a lost son?
Why shouldn't one tell a child
To leave the whetstone
When a machete advances?

Our hearts tremble
As the herds swarm
Into the fields
Slayer nomads lurking
Like midnight killers
Coming for the souls of sleepers

We pray yet as always
A visitor's presence
Should not bring death
Upon his host
And when he leaves
May hunchback
Not follow him

BEFORE WE CHOSE

Rumbling bolts and thundering threats
Draped every heart with dread
And fear dragged us along
Like a stubborn billy-goat

We flinched and trembled
We feared and quaked
Like a house nestled
On a slide-prone surface

Can you tell of any heart
That didn't conjure dirges?
Why do sinners hunger for holy war?

Time dulled the frenetic rhythm of anxiety
Mellowing our high temperature
But our mud-caked feet hold tales
Of trepidation that came with the election

Publisher's list

If you have enjoyed *This Is Not A Poem* **consider these other fine books from Mwanaka Media and Publishing:**

Cultural Hybridity and Fixity by Andrew Nyongesa
The Water Cycle by Andrew Nyongesa
Tintinnabulation of Literary Theory by Andrew Nyongesa
I Threw a Star in a Wine Glass by Fethi Sassi
South Africa and United Nations Peacekeeping Offensive Operations by Antonio Garcia
Africanization and Americanization Anthology Volume 1, Searching for Interracial, Interstitial, Intersectional and Interstates Meeting Spaces, Africa Vs North America by Tendai R Mwanaka
A Conversation..., A Contact by Tendai Rinos Mwanaka
A Dark Energy by Tendai Rinos Mwanaka
Africa, UK and Ireland: Writing Politics and Knowledge Production Vol 1 by Tendai R Mwanaka
Best New African Poets 2017 Anthology by Tendai R Mwanaka and Daniel Da Purificacao
Keys in the River: New and Collected Stories by Tendai Rinos Mwanaka
Logbook Written by a Drifter by Tendai Rinos Mwanaka
Mad Bob Republic: Bloodlines, Bile and a Crying Child by Tendai Rinos Mwanaka
How The Twins Grew Up/Makurire Akaita Mapatya by Milutin Djurickovic and Tendai Rinos Mwanaka
Writing Language, Culture and Development, Africa Vs Asia Vol 1 by Tendai R Mwanaka, Wanjohi wa Makokha and Upal Deb
Zimbolicious Poetry Vol 1 by Tendai R Mwanaka and Edward Dzonze
Zimbolicious: An Anthology of Zimbabwean Literature and Arts, Vol 3 by Tendai Mwanaka

Under The Steel Yoke by Jabulani Mzinyathi
A Case of Love and Hate by Chenjerai Mhondera
Epochs of Morning Light by Elena Botts
Fly in a Beehive by Thato Tshukudu
Bounding for Light by Richard Mbuthia
White Man Walking by John Eppel
A Cat and Mouse Affair by Bruno Shora
Sentiments by Jackson Matimba
Best New African Poets 2018 Anthology by Tendai R Mwanaka and
Nsah Mala
Drawing Without Licence by Tendai R Mwanaka
*Writing Grandmothers/ Escribiendo sobre nuestras raíces: Africa Vs Latin
America Vol 2* by Tendai R Mwanaka and Felix Rodriguez
The Scholarship Girl by Abigail George
Words That Matter by Gerry Sikazwe
The Gods Sleep Through It by Wonder Guchu
The Ungendered by Delia Watterson
The Big Noise and Other Noises by Christopher Kudyahakudadirwe
Tiny Human Protection Agency by Megan Landman
Ghetto Symphony by Mandla Mavolwane
Sky for a Foreign Bird by Fethi Sassi
A Portrait of Defiance by Tendai Rinos Mwanaka
When Escape Becomes the only Lover by Tendai R Mwanaka
Where I Belong: moments, mist and song by Smeetha Bhoumik

Soon to be released
*Nationalism: (Mis)Understanding   Donald Trump's Capitalism, Racism,
Global Politics, International Trade and Media Wars, Africa Vs North
America Vol 2* by Tendai R Mwanaka
Of Bloom Smoke by Abigail George
Denga reshiri yokunze kwenyika by Fethi Sassi

Ashes by Ken Weene and Omar O Abdul

Ouafa and Thawra: About a Lover From Tunisia by Arturo Desimone

Thoughts Hunt The Loves/Pfungwa Dzinovhima Vadiwa by Jeton Kelmendi

ويَسهَرُ اللَّيلُ عَلَى شَفَتي...وَالغَمَام by Fethi Sassi

A Letter to the President by Mbizo Chirasha

Righteous Indignation by Jabulani Mzinyathi:

Notes From a Modern Chimurenga: Collected Stories by Tendai Rinos Mwanaka

Tom Boy by Megan Landman

My Spiritual Journey: A Study of the Emerald Tablets by Jonathan Thompson

Rhythm of Life by Olivia Ngozi Osouha

Blooming Cactus By Mikateko Mbambo

Travellers Gather Dust and Lust by Gabriel Awuah Mainoo

School of Love and Other Stories by Ricardo Felix Rodriguez

Cycle of Life by Ikegwu Michael Chukwudi

https://facebook.com/MwanakaMediaAndPublishing/

Printed in the United States
By Bookmasters